Sound Activities

by Alison Saunders

WORKSHEETS

Introductory Level

EGON PUBLISHERS LTD

Royston Road, Baldock, Hertfordshire, SG7 6NW, England

First published in the United Kingdom in 1997
Second impression 1999
by Egon Publishers Ltd,
Royston Road, Baldock, Hertfordshire SG7 6NW, England

Copyright © Egon Publishers Ltd.,
and Alison Saunders, 1997

ISBN 1 899998 10 1

Origination by Climacs Imagin and printed for the publishers
by Streets Printers, Royston Road, Baldock, Hertfordshire SG7 6NW, England

INTRODUCTION

These activity sheets provide a useful resource in helping and encouraging children to develop phonic skills. They may be used by children of all abilities but are aimed particularly at the child who has difficulty in retaining sounds, who may have poor short-term memory and who would benefit from repetition and reinforcement.

Each activity offers a different, challenging and enjoyable way of reinforcing the spelling of words, helping the child to become more confident with sounds and how they link into word families.

There are three different activity sheets for each sound. These are:

1) a wordsearch
2) a 'missing words' sheet
3) a crossword puzzle

Linear Wordsearch

This has been presented in a linear format to encourage and reinforce:

◆ Sound and whole word recognition.
◆ Left to right tracking skills.
◆ Scanning skills.
◆ Hand and eye co-ordination.

It is suggested that once the child has located the word within the line of letters, it should be underlined and then the Look – Cover – Write – Check strategy be employed by writing the word at the side.

Missing Words

This is designed to encourage and reinforce:

◆ The particular sound and word family on which the activity sheet is based.
◆ Reading and Comprehension skills.
◆ Inference.
◆ The use of words in correct context and positions of words in a sentence.

The provision of answers in random order at the bottom of the activity sheet enables the less confident child to be more successful. Alternatively, the sheet can be copied without the answers if further repetition is required, or as a more advanced task.

Crossword Puzzle

This is designed to encourage and reinforce:

◆ The particular sound and word family on which the activity sheet is based.

◆ Spatial awareness and organization.

◆ Reading and Comprehension skills.

◆ The awareness and understanding of different meanings of the same word, thus extending the child's vocabulary.

◆ Self-Correction – the number of spaces indicates how many letters make the word – If a space remains, this indicates that a letter has been omitted – if not enough spaces remain then too many letters have been inserted.

◆ Logical thinking. Existing letters can be used to help solve another clue.

◆ Shared Reading. One child reads the clues across and another reads the clues down. This also encourages the sharing of ideas and helping each other.

Similarly the answers are provided at the bottom of the activity sheet. The sheet can also be copied without the answers if further repetition is required, or as a more advanced task.

These sheets have been piloted at Breakspear Junior School, Ickenham, which is in the London Borough of Hillingdon, where I am the Special Needs Co-ordinator. Children have worked on the sheets on their own and with the help of Louise Lipscombe to whom I am most grateful for her help and suggestions. They have been used by pupils in Years 3, 4 and 5 but could probably be tackled by more able pupils in Year 2. A further use has emerged as useful material for pupils for whom English is an additional language.

I have been grateful too for the advice and encouragement of Mrs Violet Brand in preparing these worksheets.

Alison Saunders Dip. RSA

Missing Words

1. The black _____ sat up in the tree.

2. We had _____ to eat for tea.

3. Mum has a big _____ to go to the shops.

4. I have a red _____ that I put on when it is cold.

5. Sam is _____ as he has lost his ball.

6. Dad has an old _____ to wipe the car.

7. One of the pigs ate a lot and was very _____ .

8. We _____ at the table to have tea.

9. We _____ up the road to get to school.

10. The old _____ takes his dog for a walk.

cat   hat   fat   sat   sad

man   ran   ham   bag   rag

1. datojaterofatirist

2. ganuraniplonijan

3. gadutadobagopag

4. sadivadegatsafam

5. scafolaticaducatep

6. sarusatimahaipafub

7. kamuhabihajauhatid

8. hafonadihamuhabufa

9. crafudarpabafuragke

10. bavmanikamilalacag

cat	hat	fat	sat	sad
man	ran	ham	bag	rag

Name....................................

Date....................................

Across

1. Cold meat.

2. The boy _____ on a chair.

4. A small animal that is a pet.

Down

1. You put this on your head.

2. Not happy.

3. The man was very _____ .

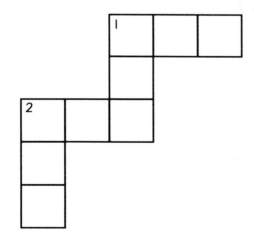

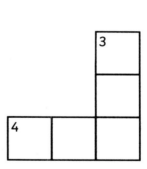

sat   ham   cat

fat   hat   sad

Missing Words

1. The baby went to sleep in the _____.

2. You must _____ and look before you cross the road.

3. It was a _____ day so we had a swim.

4. The _____ shelf was too high to reach.

5. I like to _____ on my left foot.

6. The _____ crept into the woods at night.

7. The _____ kept on barking.

8. _____ Saturday we will go to the shops.

9. The chair was hard to sit on, not _____.

10. The _____ was full of toys.

dog   cot   hot   top   hop

stop   box   fox   on   soft

<u>Wordsearch</u>

1. sromdoprukoflugopdog

2. palokrtoxdehotkihrsev

3. trostokcistopifhuylomg

4. serhozsoftgrehpolumo

5. fohokflovdoprtecohopo

6. tetocdfolasdtyboxpxthig

7. drovoctopdeoprokoquaft

8. cotbreskopfribozscojeow

9. groyflunfoxpogegycomipt

10. desrogsovocrohosdsocbkon

dog	cot	hot	top	hop
stop	box	fox	on	soft

Name..

Date..

Across

1. A baby sleeps in this.

3. To jump on one foot.

4. An animal that barks.

6. Not cold.

Down

2. Not under the table but on _____.

5. Not hard.

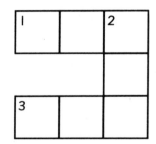

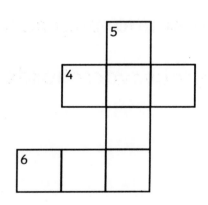

hop   dog   hot

cot   top   soft

Name................................

Date................................

1. I _____ the ball very hard.

2. The _____ blew in the trees.

3. The bad dog _____ a hole in the slipper.

4. My sister has _____ dolls.

5. We sailed on a _____ boat to France.

6. The fat, pink _____ lives on the farm.

7. I hope that my football team _____ the game.

8. Sam's Mum took _____ to the zoo.

9. Emma likes to _____ and watch the TV.

10. My Mum puts on pink _____ stick.

big   bit   hit   sit   lip

him   pig   six   win   wind

1. drirwstizegrisigiclibigu

2. flakigmiligomipigsruct

3. tixyunixdefsixfsywecil

4. lokilsminbahrerliptirup

5. chigtiboigisblvithitoch

6. shiruwstoniwrinlahimest

7. sicdflerikirdslijwindgrih

8. blihstupbityoligrisluvrin

9. vinfrimsligexipsitiohjuyb

10. wemigcitpeywibepwinist

big	bit	hit	sit	lip
him	pig	six	win	wind

Across

1. Part of the mouth.

3. Not small.

5. 4 + 2 =

Down

2. A pink farm animal.

3. The box was a _____ too small for all the toys.

4. He _____ the ball.

big   bit   pig

hit   lip   six

Missing Words

1. The _____ laid an egg.

2. The ball was _____ and blue.

3. I can stand on one _____ .

4. I _____ for a long time and did not want to wake up.

5. I have _____ toes .

6. In June we _____ away to stay with Gran.

7. The old lady needed _____ to cross the road.

8. The robin made a _____ in the tree.

9. Mum said, "It is not _____ time for tea."

10. After tea, Mum said it was time for _____.

bed   hen   leg   red   ten

yet   help   nest   went   slept

Wordsearch

1. scadfrenkiheptenrusdem

2. esmestremiberihesimnest

3. slunigerargepweveptslept

4. yunyudelaseyetihevegiprt

5. brefbedsefbepuitrlebeaxch

6. cholihegtreghusfoleredatish

7. sterwoulefipwentepresemot

8. fudelihepreshibhehovhenim

9. jhebpolgebpibhelpontrecem

10. lebikoheleclegrelepuvserthu

bed	hen	leg	red	ten
yet	help	nest	went	slept

Crossword

Across

1. 5 + 5 =

4. He _____ in bed.

6. A colour.

Down

2. Birds lay eggs here.

3. The boy shouted for _____ .

5. You sleep in this.

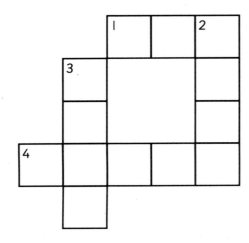

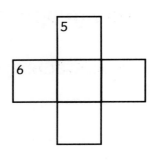

nest   red   ten   bed

slept   nest   help

Missing Words

1. We went by _____ to the shops.

2. We had to _____ up and down to keep warm.

3. The balloon went _____ in the sky.

4. It is _____ to go to the park.

5. Mr. Smith had to _____ to catch the train.

6. He _____ not be late for work.

7. The boys ran in the _____ and were very dirty.

8. The _____ is hot in summer.

9. Grandma likes to have a _____ of tea.

10. Jane is ill with _____.

bus   cup   fun   sun   mud

jump   run   up   must   mumps

Wordsearch

u

1. truxlespuzthripelebusrertrew

2. stursohinfivwemisundeopytrij

3. mijkiopujumpretulupuystoger

4. muhunbretidacomumpsefivug

5. utyrecderopimcupicresuvipret

6. riwrunoperthicaguhukipaferiob

7. nufermuytrabicamustosuruyute

8. renenuhukixerstefunimolufotuy

9. cuvukertuhibuvumuditecesgug

10. crefutoricipekibuweruprulhars

bus   cup   fun   sun   mud

jump   run   up   must   mumps

Name ....

Date ....

Crossword

Across

2. The boy fell in the wet _____ .

3. A _____ of tea.

6. It shines in the sky.

Down

1. The dog can _____ over the gate.

4. Not down.

5. I can _____ fast.

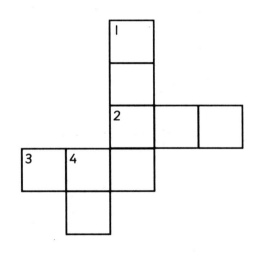

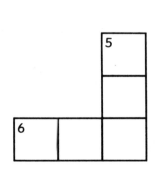

mud   run   cup

jump   sun   up

Name.................................

Date.................................

ck

1. I lost a _____under the bed.

2. Sally likes to _____ a sweet from the box.

3. James can _____ a ball very hard.

4. It is good to _____ an ice-cream.

5. I cut out a picture and had to _____ it in my book.

6. The boat was _____ in the mud.

7. Tom slipped and fell _____ on the floor.

8. The swan has a long _____.

9. We went _____ to school on Monday.

10. The boy was _____ so he had to stay at home.

back   lick   kick   pick   neck

sick   sock   stick   stuck   smack

1.   gickhuckackpickuyerck

2.   leckopultejickfickasock

3.   juckobockusickpruhuck

4.   steckibackupleckertyock

5.   smarsmackuckilweckurt

6.   vuckisteckijoquckostick

7.   dackuckickouphuckmec

8.   stuckoplegickubreckeck

9.   dackuneleckuneckijecke

10.   guckiolokuweckugivlick

back   lick   kick   pick   neck

sick   sock   stick   stuck   smack

Across

2. You put this on your foot.

3. Sam can ____ the ball.

5. You must not ____ the flowers.

Down

1. John sat in the _____ of the car.

2. This comes from a tree.

4. Sally and Jane ____ pink ice creams.

kick   sock   back

lick   stick   pick

1. The _____ at the end of the garden was green.

2. I had to _____ my Dad at three o'clock.

3. Sam needed new shoes as his _____ had grown.

4. In the park, it said, " _____ off the grass."

5. The baby went to _____ at six o'clock.

6. "Have you _____ my new bike?" Tom asked.

7. Emma's dress is pink and _____ .

8. We went to _____ the new film.

9. The jam tart was very _____ .

10. I had a comic and there was a _____ pen with it.

feet   *see*   *meet*   *tree*   *free*

green   *keep*   *sleep*   *sweet*   *seen*

Name ....

Date ....

1. grethneescereeguptkedutreesp

2. kregrisereeburveempekeesleep

3. sreethalorineesweetruceepims

4. creehuveeirgreenojesdeegheen

5. cleemiveecreskimofreebosteree

6. steebokideegokeeporusneemoln

7. creefikeegomeetofisreebipheen

8. deregeelomictireeseenoheebosug

9. lomelefeekrafeetpilogeetureerast

10. dreespoliseehunipreegukarixeert

feet	see	meet	tree	free
green	keep	sleep	sweet	seen

Name..

Date...

Crossword

ee

Across

3. It grows in a wood.

4. She went to bed to ____ .

5. A colour.

Down

1. We had to ____ at 3 o'clock.

2. I must ____ my work tidy.

4. The apple was _____ .

meet   tree   keep

green   sleep   sweet

Missing Words

1. The baby eats his food with a _____ .

2. We went to the _____ to see the lions.

3. Up in the sky, the _____ was shining.

4. Jim wants to _____ eggs for tea.

5. Sam kicks the ball with his left _____ .

6. Before you cross the road you must _____ both ways.

7. At the party we had a _____ time.

8. Is there _____ for me to sit on the bench?

9. We went to the shops to buy some _____ for the weekend.

10. The sun has gone and it will _____ be dark.

room   soon   spoon

look   foot   good

1. foopidookibooduspoonar

2. roohuvoosazooperinoomip

3. frinoodomoonarihoolathom

4. groonimasoonurekoobesool

5. rewodoodakooburoomonoot

6. coomikooseradoopicookiral

7. darogimahooniresigoodatho

8. flooberinoofootirusuhupoom

9. kimudoohuvigoolerethofood

10. lookimejoofimafoocroobasc

food   moon   room   soon   spoon

zoo   cook   look   foot   good

Across

2. It will ____ be time for tea.

4. Mum can ____ food.

5. It shines at night.

Down

1. You do this with your eyes.

2. You eat with this.

3. I sleep in my _____ .

cook   look   moon

room   soon   spoon

Missing Words

1. I took a spoon of jam from the _____ .

2. In the sky, a bright _____ was shining.

3. The dog will _____ when he sees a cat.

4. Sally put on a _____ as it was cold.

5. We went to school in the _____ .

6. Gran made an apple _____ for lunch.

7. We went by bus to the swimming pool as it was too _____ to walk.

8. It was getting _____, so we had to put on the light.

9. Sam had to pay to _____ the car.

10. It was cold and the car did not want to _____ .

car   far   park   dark   jar

star   bark   tart   scarf   start

1. storarinaropulariharostar

2. bikarltuparickelarojares

3. haromurisariscarfiporile

4. wahiborarileparkikoelar

5. sropucarhinaropecsarth

6. varoparlsarulonarstartm

7. faruvarinysturaruwobirc

8. stercrofudarivarscuntart

9. mibarkelopersarlefrarkib

10. durkiharudarkiyarulonp

car   far   park   dark   jar

star   bark   tart   scarf   start

Name.....................................

Date.....................................

Across

2. It keeps you warm.

4. The dogs began to _____ .

5. A jam _____ .

Down

1. Not light.

2. To begin.

3. A long way away.

start   dark   bark

scarf   far   tart

Introductory Level   27

Missing Words

1.   We use a knife and _____ to eat our lunch.

2.   Which _____ of sweets do you like ?

3.   On Sunday, Mum cooked some _____ for lunch.

4.   We looked _____ shells by the sea.

5.   The _____ was bad and it was raining hard.

6.   It was a good harvest and there were
     fields of _____ .

7.   On Saturday, Jenny likes to go _____ riding.

8.   When were you _____ ?

9.   Peter and Sally play a lot of _____ .

10. Dad took the _____ out of the bottle.

fork   cork   pork   corn   born

for   horse   storm   sport   sort

Name...

Date...

or

1. dortuvaroreshorseporpuv

2. cojorstumorhariorporkes

3. shonsportirukorebalorpsh

4. ferorechormirborgastormi

5. fefotamaforkoperiortesdy

6. klefuhortchorgabornistch

7. tiornusdorlorcornoporfim

8. clornasiorucorkelormasny

9. ferforopihormilctikonoper

10. shorchorgerahoshusortauh

fork   cork   pork   corn   born

for   horse   storm   sport   sort

Crossword

Across

2. An animal.

4. You eat with this.

6. Rain and strong wind.

Down

1. Meat from a pig.

3. Games like football and tennis.

5. Peter was _____ seven years ago.

storm   fork   pork

sport   born   horse

Missing Words

1. John went to the _____ to buy a paper.

2. We had _____ and chips for dinner.

3. It was late and we had to _____ to school.

4. The gate was _____ to stop the animals getting out.

5. We had to be careful as the knife was _____ .

6. On the high field there were _____ and lambs.

7. The glass _____ was full of sweets.

8. It was my birthday and I made a _____ .

9. I have a blue _____ on my bed.

10. The _____ set sail at seven o'clock.

shop   shut   sheep   sharp   ship

fish   dish   wish   rush   sheet

Name.............................. **Wordsearch**

Date..............................

1. shuvoshicdisharoshiker

2. sharisheeporshertushib

3. wushifosharusharishory

4. hichaluishomawushopur

5. scugopeshanesharpilkish

6. ershanishujishepibeshuty

7. sctushifishuseshiklomishp

8. weshuvioreshiwishiloshuh

9. shuhikeriheshibeshipobesh

10. shishuplisheetushoishereash

shop   shut   sheep   sharp   ship

fish   dish   wish   rush   sheet

Name.....................................

Date.....................................

Across

2. The gate was not open but _____ .

3. It swims in the sea.

4. We had to _____ to get to the shops.

Down

1. You put food in this.

2. An animal that gives us wool.

5. You buy food at the _____.

shop   shut   sheep

rush   dish   fish

Name..

Date..

1. On Friday we all had fish and _____ to eat.

2. I asked how _____ the toy was.

3. Sam likes to _____ a bag of crisps.

4. We saw the soldiers_____ past.

5. Mum stopped to _____ to the lady next door.

6. On the side of the plate was a _____ .

7. The farmer has an axe to _____ the wood.

8. We were making a pie and added
    a _____ of salt.

9. James fell and bumped his _____ .

10. The boxer used a _____ bag.

chin   chip   chips   chat   chop

much   pinch   punch   munch   march

Wordsearch

1. dirchuyichafuchaturesich

2. jikupinchusecitchudoper

3. decetibimarchufutcharsy

4. cunchaxurchikomunchirs

5. chifamichikolachipiduch

6. homuchafubechertisedoch

7. dechuromacheclomichips

8. juchimautichudochinostp

9. drochuyeplochupurupunch

10. struchagimochopikunacher

chin   chip   chips   chat   chop

much   pinch   punch   munch   march

Name................................

Date................................

ch

Across

2. He likes to _____ the apple.

4. There was too _____ water in the jug.

5. To hit hard with the fist.

Down

1. A part of the face.

3. To cut wood with an axe.

4. A month of the year.

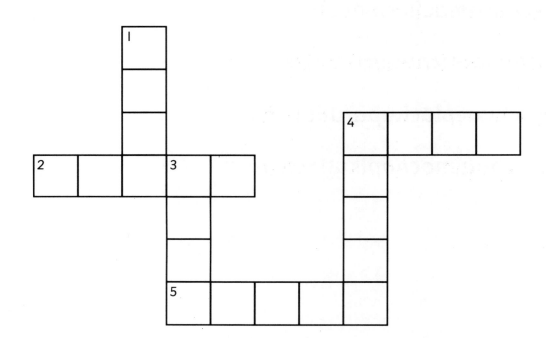

chop   chin   much

March   munch   punch

1. The tree grew very tall and _____ .

2. My little sister will be _____ on her next birthday.

3. Sam went _____ Tom to the sweet shop.

4. Emma said, "_____ you for lending me your book."

5. I asked my Mum, "Do you _____ it will rain?"

6. _____ pencil is longer than mine.

7. We went to the woods and _____ climbed the trees.

8. "_____ new coat is smart," said the lady.

9. We went out with our friends and bought _____ each an ice-cream.

10. My dog is older _____ your dog.

thin   think   thank   three   that

then   this   them   than   with

<u>Wordsearch</u>

1. thurexusthilputhreebuth

2. dehiblothuyedotrhiwithy

3. scilomuthunitharuthinkop

4. sthafothikothafethatolosck

5. thufecikothiumarthanepak

6. threfoputhuvesyuthemipol

7. shrithuveceathisedruthoick

8. dlothankiboudesthiwanaith

9. brauthuhusholuthenaerstcah

10. festethabocthiwiolthinujisth

thin	think	thank	three	that
then	this	them	than	with

Name..

Date..

Crossword

Across

2. This crossword makes me _____ .

3. Will you play ball ____ me?

4. _____ you for my birthday present.

Down

1. Not fat.

2. The sun came out and _____ we went to the park.

4. A number.

with   then   thin

think   thank   three

Missing Words

a e

1. We played a good _____ of tennis.

2. You must shut the _____ when you leave the field.

3. I made a chocolate _____ for tea.

4. John must _____ his money to buy a new football.

5. I packed my _____ to go on holiday.

6. My brother wants to have a pet _____ .

7. There was a big _____ of cakes.

8. Sally cut the card in the _____ of a bird.

9. If I look up, I can see the _____ high up in the sky.

10. It was hot and Mum _____ me a drink.

cake   case   game   gate   made

plane   shape   snake   save   plate

Date...

1. cadroucedaudegamekapre

2. plaberukesnakelokerthune

3. strabeuthunesplatepakersy

4. maberuveplaneugesyeruve

5. cideoplaveneumeicasehie

6. chedeirivemunesavegreceb

7. strefepameuvateshaneshape

8. cakeujapetrafelyasethaigery

9. glaseseaderabelahegatepame

10. gadetvakewapeclerfayemade

cake   case   game   gate   made

plane   shape   snake   save   plate

Crossword

a e

Across

1. The cake is a round _____ .

2. We had cherry _____ for tea.

3. The _____ was open and the dog ran out.

Down

1. An animal with a very long body.

2. We took a big _____ on holiday.

3. I saw a _____ of football.

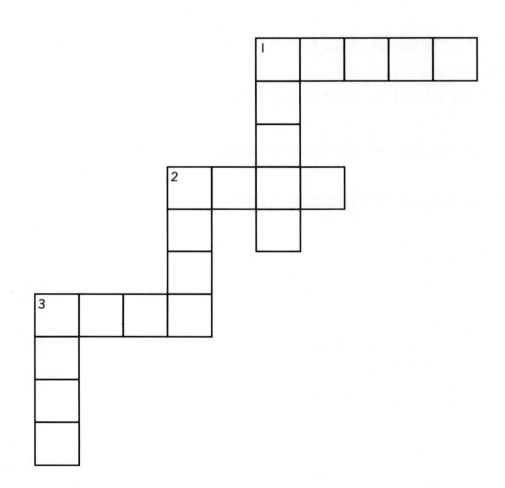

cake   case   gate

game   snake   shape

Missing Words

ie

1. Now my brother is _____, he goes to school.

2. At the park, there are swings and a _____ .

3. I hope the sun will _____ and we can go out to play.

4. Mum put _____ in the drink to make it cool.

5. Mark took a big _____ from the apple.

6. I _____ going swimming with my friends.

7. There were ten sweets in the packet but I ate one so that left _____ .

8. Tom can ride very fast on his new _____ .

9. I looked at the clock as I did not know the _____ .

10. The farmer's _____ helps to milk the cows.

bike   bite   five   nine   like

time   slide   shine   wife   ice

Wordsearch

1. piteubivewimegizebite

2. liwepijetivefivepoiker

3. hibesibecehigenyicefip

4. stidwiberixeshineliges

5. lisewertibetimedoperst

6. vikeryunikepafebikefl

7. cinedyilomibeslidekile

8. awriwifegilertikethilem

9. cliseticheoparlikesturey

10. mifegorigeninefidepibe

bike   bite   five   nine   like

time   slide   shine   wife   ice

Name ....

Date ....

Crossword

ie

Across

2. The street lamps _____ at night.

3. The _____ is 4 o'clock.

5. It has two wheels and you can ride it.

Down

1. 3 x 3 =

2. I went down the _____ in the park.

4. A number less than six.

time   five   bike

shine   slide   nine

Missing Words

o e

1. Jane told me a _____ which made me laugh.

2. The dog's _____ felt very cold.

3. Firemen came as there was _____ coming from the house.

4. The children like to climb the _____ .

5. Tim was upset when his new toy _____ .

6. Our dog likes to chew a _____ .

7. The red _____ smells very sweet.

8. At the end of the day, it was time to go _____ .

9. I knocked my big _____ on the table leg.

10. We went out and I had an ice-cream _____ .

home   joke   nose   rose   toe

bone   cone   rope   smoke   broke

Wordsearch

o e

1. yomerstobersothiropev

2. dobeunsmokepomestch

3. flomersfocheconekertle

4. strocherokebrokebixest

5. boenoketoefumopofech

6. koletrosenolertstochery

7. cobertfolejoledronajoke

8. hoberstobejonerschome

9. lokeroceybonedrokersy

10. mokerocenoserdobesge

home   joke   nose   rose   toe

bone   cone   rope   smoke   broke

Name ....

Crossword

o e

Date ....

Across

2. You smell with this.

4. The cup fell off the shelf and ____ .

5. Each foot has a big ____ .

Down

1. A flower.

3. There was a lot of ____ coming from the fire.

4. The dog hid the ____ in the garden.

toe   rose   nose

bone   broke   smoke

Missing Words

1. It was a summer's day and the sky was _____ .

2. I could not do the puzzle and asked for a _____ .

3. At school, we always have Sports day in _____ .

4. We had to buy a new _____ of toothpaste.

5. James needed some _____ to stick his model together.

6. The books must go back to the library on _____ .

7. Sally was playing a _____ on her recorder.

8. There was a _____ spider running across the floor.

9. The teacher told the children off for being _____ .

10. At school we have a _____ that you must not run inside.

blue   June   tune   tube   rude

clue   glue   rule   huge   Tuesday

Wordsearch

1. kugeruvebluesturethelk

2. guberuveoludeotunepul

3. yuneopertubeluchucerm

4. lujeruvehugepugesupem

5. clunerukecruperuletruke

6. JumerukeJunelomiJucen

7. nujeclupestukecluekume

8. TukerujopsiTuesdayTuv

9. kumerudefuberoplutcher

10. plutheryunerglubescglue

blue   June   tune   tube   rude

clue   glue   rule   huge   Tuesday

Crossword

u e

Across

3. You use this to stick paper.

4. A day of the week.

5. A colour.

Down

1. Very big.

2. We looked for a _____ to help us find the prize.

4. A _____ of toothpaste.

blue   clue   glue

huge   tube   Tuesday

1.   We went by _____ to London.

2.   The _____ went slowly along the path.

3.   We had to _____ a long time for the bus.

4.   I fell over and then had a _____ in my leg.

5.   The boat was tied to the post with a _____.

6.   Dad has some new _____ for the front door.

7.   The pig's _____ is very curly.

8.   It began to _____ so we did not go out.

9.   The boat had a large white _____ .

10.   Gran held on to the _____ as she went
     up the steps.

rain   train   rail   tail   sail

snail   pain   chain   paint   wait

1.   naistaiferailitechaiger

2.   spaichaisteraibaifpain

3.   haidertaisefotrainomor

4.   thainaristaichosnailaisp

5.   jaitchainopaiteronaiker

6.   caidobreshowaitikailtoh

7.   slaifutshainerainomusaip

8.   luplaiguherosaikepaintic

9.   kaidoflaiseraijaiyutailuser

10. skaiceraifujaimosailomin

rain	train	rail	tail	sail
snail	pain	chain	paint	wait

Crossword

ai

Across

2. I have a _____ in my leg.

3. An animal with a hard shell.

4. We went by bus and _____ .

6. She wore a gold _____ .

Down

1. Our cat likes to swish his _____ .

2. I like to _____ pictures.

5. We got wet in the _____ .

rain   chain   train

pain   paint   tail   snail

Missing Words

1. I put on my _____ as it was cold.

2. Jenny had two slices of _____ for breakfast.

3. Mark used _____ to wash his face.

4. The wood began to _____ along the river.

5. Mum bought a _____ of bread from the bakers.

6. We live on a busy _____ .

7. We gave a huge _____ as we had to tidy our bedrooms.

8. We sailed across the lake in a small _____ .

9. There was a heavy _____ of shopping to bring home.

10. Our team soon scored a _____ in the game.

boat   coat   road   load   loaf

toast   soap   groan   float   goal

1. doaleroapimoasloafert

2. coafloashiroadoanachy

3. hoalospoadutoaboatush

4. voadumoasefloatupoath

5. broasotoaloperoagroano

6. junoastumoaxosloatoast

7. spoalikoasoipaisoapolie

8. cloaproasicoatjoaducoam

9. floahroanuboaseroloadeko

10. cloawugoaluhoasteroafulp

boat	coat	road	load	loaf
toast	soap	groan	float	goal

Name..

Date..

Across

1. A _____ of bread.

3. Our school is on a main ____ .

4. We had hot _____ for tea.

Down

1. The _____ was very heavy.

2. The sticks will ____ on the water.

5. We use _____ to wash.

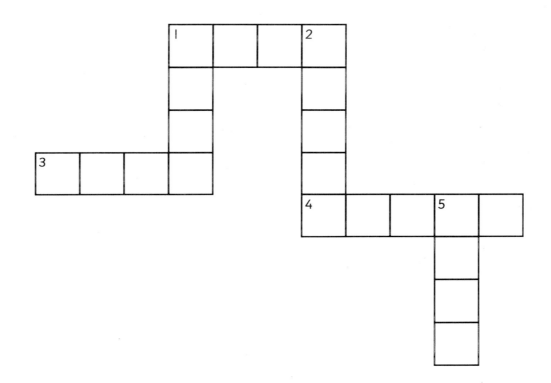

load   road   loaf

soap   float   toast

Missing Words

1. A _____ singing outside woke me up.

2. James had a white _____ for school.

3. Emma's new school _____ was long.

4. Sally was the _____ in the race.

5. Peter walked down the lane and got _____ on his shoes.

6. Tom will be ten on his next _____ .

7. The _____ tree had a lot of cones.

8. The _____ who lives next door, has long hair.

9. We had to wipe the windows as they were very _____.

10. Mum asked me to _____ the soup in the pan.

girl   bird   stir   skirt   shirt

fir   dirt   dirty   first   birthday

Name ....

Date ....

Wordsearch

1. cirltirbrescushirtopirm

2. kirstuniropirnogirleps

3. virutibirdushirgirchon

4. plirdunirstavirnskirtirt

5. drirtunirchostirpirkolir

6. birshucibirtunebirthday

7. striruviropirstufirstimirt

8. drirpolirtumirchoudirtam

9. kiruniromirasofirujirtoresy

10. girtudirtyolirtyolirsihirtyer

girl   bird   stir   skirt   shirt

fir   dirt   dirty   first   birthday

Name...

Date...

Across

2. The ____ made a nest.

4. The girl had a blue ____ .

5. Jane will be nine on her next_____ .

6. She came ____ in the race.

Down

1. The wood had lots of ____ trees.

3. There was ____ on John's coat when he played in the mud.

4. The boy had on a red_____ .

fir   first   bird   dirt

skirt   shirt   birthday

Missing Words

1. There was a dark _____ and it began to rain.

2. There was a _____ bang from the fireworks.

3. The _____ ran across the garden path.

4. The _____ has three bedrooms.

5. Last week at school, we _____ the ball that we had lost.

6. The apples fell from the tree to the _____ .

7. I was hiding from my friend and went _____ to the back of the house.

8. As we ran in the woods we had to look _____ for logs across the path.

9. We went to the library to find out _____ our town.

10. I had to _____ to my friend as he was a long way away.

cloud   loud   round   found   ground

shout   out   about   house   mouse

Wordsearch

1. ploushoumoukiroundaw

2. houneropoumousecoush

3. stouwilounicloudiloumer

4. vounimoulasousheground

5. foupikounyeroufoundroug

6. maboushanougrouliaboute

7. voushokoumilouchohousen

8. jounimouclousifouteromiry

9. dirloudimounistoulerikouge

10. cloukanoushabouderishoutik

cloud   loud   round   found   ground

shout   out   about   house   mouse

Across

1. A white _____ was in the sky.

4. The apple fell to the _____ .

6. The cat ran after the _____.

Down

2. The music was very _____ .

3. Our _____ has a new roof.

5. We live _____ the corner from our school.

loud   cloud   house

round   mouse   ground

Name ....
Date ....
<u>Missing Words</u>

ea (ē)

1. For lunch we cooked the _____ in the oven.

2. Sam and Tom like baked _____ on toast.

3. Granny likes to have a cup of _____ in the afternoon.

4. We went swimming in the _____ which was warm.

5. We found lots of shells on the _____.

6. Last night I had a funny _____.

7. In the park, we sat on the _____ for a rest.

8. We had to cook the _____ in a pan for five minutes.

9. There was a jug of _____ on the table.

10. We went on an outing and took a packed lunch to _____.

eat	meat	peas	beans	cream
tea	sea	seat	beach	dream

Name......................................

Date......................................

ea (ē)

1. feaduleasimeagudreamuv

2. ceanumeapeseajubeashure

3. clopreafikeamibeachoyea

4. lomeasufeashicreamikead

5. sleabukeadokeagarseatict

6. deashneadileagimeatuchep

7. brealupeasimeashouleam

8. clikuneasheajuckeatomeab

9. croibeagubeaveleathubeans

10. teafolealimoukeneacuneady

eat   meat   peas   beans   cream

tea   sea   seat   beach   dream

Name..

Date..

Crossword

ea (ē)

Across

2. I like to _____ cream cakes.

4. You sit on this.

5. The sand by the sea is called the _____ .

Down

1. We had roast _____ .

3. A hot drink.

4. We swam in the _____ .

6. _____ is made from milk.

sea   tea   eat

meat   seat   beach   cream

Missing Words

1. My friend is coming to _____ for tea.

2. On _____ afternoon we all went out.

3. Last year we went _____ for two weeks
    to the sea.

4. In the month of _____ there are lots
    of Spring flowers out.

5. On _____ each week we have Art at school.

6. Did you _____ that you had seen my coat?

7. We had to _____ to park the car.

8. On the TV, I heard that it will rain _____ .

9. We hope to _____ a football match next week.

10. I like to go on _____ in the summer when
    it is hot.

play   pay   say   stay   today

holiday   away   May   Sunday   Tuesday

1. tayriaysteyloyplayovayer

2. steayruykayireayiayostay

3. awirovayufayiawayuxay

4. SouylerSfaySolunSunday

5. hoaylelpokayuiayholiday

6. peshyayeruyayvayipayuay

7. MaMeuynayMercayMay

8. tofeaytoayotodayulofaytiy

9. ThusdayTorseayTuesday

10. zayuaycayiayosayinloay

play   pay   say   stay   today

holiday   away   May   Sunday   Tuesday

Name...................................

Date....................................

Crossword

Across

1. How much do I _____ for the book?

2. The first day of the week.

3. The day after Monday.

5. A month of the year.

Down

1. Will you _____ a game with me?

2. We went to _____ for three nights.

4. "What did you _____ ?" said Mum.

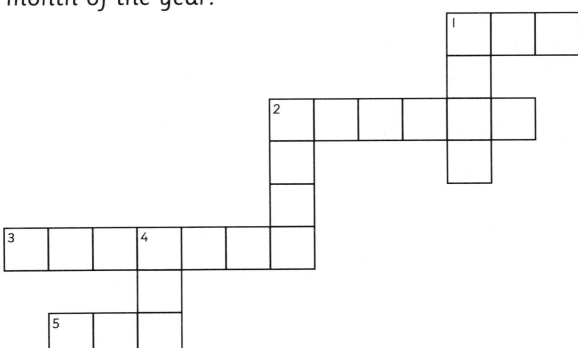

pay   say   May   Sunday

stay   play   Tuesday

1. While Mum was _____ the car we went
    in the sweet shop.

2. I was_____ for my pencil as I had lost it.

3. John is _____ with his new game.

4. The cat was _____ on a rug in front
    of the fire.

5. We are _____ at our friend's house
    for the weekend.

6. I could smell that lunch was _____
    in the kitchen.

7. We were _____ for a long time in the
    shop waiting to pay.

8. Last Saturday my sister and I were _____
    Dad to wash the car.

9. I was _____ about lots of snow falling
    in Winter.

10. At the show, the horses were _____ over
    the fences.

playing   staying   helping   sleeping   cooking

looking   standing   parking   dreaming   jumping

1. junindocingaplayinguhing

2. huningojingahelpinguling

3. kolingingbingcitingcooking

4. lingavingrtingiparkingubing

5. sedingeningstayingipolkinge

6. tremingucingjolingarlooking

7. striguingalingkibingsleeping

8. stelingenistandingingopeing

9. clomingelingedreamingying

10. chuningpagjumpingingming

playing   staying   helping   sleeping   cooking

looking   standing   parking   dreaming   jumping

Name..................................

Date..................................

Across

1. The cat was _____ by the fire.

3. The soldiers were _____ still.

5. The boys were _____ in the park.

6. I was _____ Dad to clean the car.

Down

2. Mum was _____ the car.

4. Last night I was _____ about being rich.

dreaming   sleeping   standing

playing   parking   helping

Missing Words

1. On Sunday we saw people coming out of _____ .

2. Sam fell over and _____ his knee.

3. The door _____ open as the children ran in from the garden.

4. On _____ we shall be going to a party.

5. We have to walk down the road and _____ left to go to school.

6. Sally goes swimming every week on a _____ .

7. For Christmas dinner we ate roast _____ .

8. I saw the hedgehog begin to _____ up into a ball.

9. When the cat sits on my lap, I stroke his _____ .

10. I can see the flames as the fire begins to _____ .

church   burn   fur   hurt   curl

turn   burst   Saturday Thursday turkey

Name.............................

Date.............................

1. nurtipurtojurtchurchctur

2. jurstipurgiburstolurtiurt

3. burmicurnodurnaturkey

4. gurilinurtimurkafurokur

5. vurnopurmikursherlturn

6. licsmurtoupimcurlchurm

7. SatdaySathuerdaySaturday

8. hurnikurceihurtoloukiryurb

9. ThuesdayThurdayThursday

10. vurtonurmihurkiluraburnur

church   burn   fur   hurt   turn

curl   burst   turkey   Saturday   Thursday

Name.....................................

Date.....................................

Crossword

Across

2. The balloon _____ .

4. One of the days at the weekend.

6. The fire began to _____ .

Down

1. Meat that you eat at Christmas.

3. The day before Friday.

5. I had to _____ the key to open the door.

turn   burn   Thursday

burst   turkey   Saturday

Missing Words

1. Tim gave a big _____ as he was sleepy.

2. I looked at the ants _____ across the path.

3. The cat held out his _____ to be stroked.

4. Our rabbit likes to eat _____ carrots.

5. Sam fell and hit his _____ on the table.

6. The _____ was green and had just been cut.

7. Anne drank a milkshake with a _____ .

8. We went to the circus and _____ the clowns.

9. At school we had to _____ a picture
   of our house.

10. At the zoo I saw the lion's sharp _____ .

yawn   saw   jaw   claw   draw

lawn   crawl   paw   raw   straw

1. fawobawijawirogawim

2. jickawofawovawisawilp

3. kawnoriwawnistimlawn

4. glawmawrihedrawirovaw

5. snawerpimawtihvawclaw

6. pawericaitoawivawakawn

7. burtostrecikawunawustraw

8. vawerstuawnawirawscikaw

9. mawnuawbiyawnolertawter

10. lokawmawticrawlokawlimuy

yawn   saw   jaw   claw   draw

lawn   crawl   paw   raw   straw

Across

2. The animals slept on the _____ .

3. The bird has a sharp _____ .

4. The green_____ was flat to play on.

Down

1. Food that is not cooked is _____ .

2. We _____ a good film.

3. The baby can _____ .

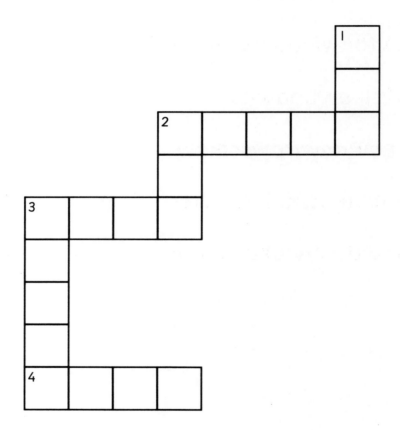

saw   raw   straw

claw   lawn   crawl

Missing Words

1. In my pocket I found a new 10p _____ .

2. We had to _____ the beans for ten minutes.

3. Emma asked if she could _____ in the game.

4. It was hard work digging the _____ .

5. The new pencil has a very sharp _____ .

6. You must take care when painting so you do not _____ the picture.

7. Dad had to put a can of _____ in the car.

8. I like it when we have a _____ of meat to eat.

9. We made stars out of silver _____ .

10. There was a lot of _____ from the party.

point   join   joint   coin   oil

foil   soil   spoil   boil   noise

1. noikoloiguboimahoigoil

2. woimoiseboisuverinoise

3. coikujoitoikoicoinuerm

4. rointumoinepointimoikst

5. moikuboimujoibspoiluc

6. voikuhoikesoilujoikuvoip

7. troiruhoijoibenijoimujoin

8. floipufoilumoideroinume

9. loipujoibiyoifuboilutoike

10. goikaujoidoivujointujoich

point   join   joint   coin   oil

foil   soil   spoil   boil   noise

Crossword

Across

1. I am going to _____ the swimming club.

3. The _____ of the pin was sharp.

4. Mum put the kettle on to _____ .

Down

1. The old man's knee _____ hurt.

2. You must not _____ your new shoes.

5. We put _____ in the pan to fry the chips.

oil   boil   spoil

join   joint   point

<u>Missing Words</u>

1. I found my slipper _____ the bed.

2. On _____ 5th we went to a firework party.

3. My _____ has the bedroom next to mine.

4. I wrote a _____ to say thank you for
my present.

5. _____ we could not go out to play as it
was raining.

6. In _____ it is always cold and the days
are short.

7. In _____ it is hot and it gets dark late in
the evening.

8. We had a hot chocolate drink and cake for _____ .

9. In _____ I will go into a new class at school.

10. There is a long play at _____ time.

dinner   supper   sister   letter   winter

summer   under   yesterday   September   November

1.   lemerusperuwinteripolter

2.   verteruyegertifayesterday

3.   vuismitisushericistersister

4.   bippertiloperletterujudetter

5.   SepretumerSuberSeptember

6.   kinneruhikkerdinnereturrer

7.   vindroyunderdulkerovinder

8.   sopperimusserpasupperolper

9.   NovmberNoverberNovember

10.   suvverpommerulperusummer

dinner   supper   sister   letter   winter

summer   under   yesterday   September   November

Name ....

Date ....

Crossword

Across

1. It is cold in _____ .

4. The month before October.

5. I wrote a _____ to my Grandma.

Down

2. The month after October.

3. An evening meal.

4. I have an older _____ .

winter   letter   September

sister   supper   November

Missing Words

1. Tom scored a goal at the _____ match.

2. The tree in the park grew very _____ .

3. At Christmas we put on a play in the school _____ .

4. At the end of our garden is a very high _____ .

5. "I will _____ you when it's time for tea," Mum said.

6. _____ the children go swimming on a Tuesday.

7. We bought some apples at the market _____ .

8. The leaves began to _____ from the trees.

9. Jane hit the tennis _____ over the net.

10. Our puppy is _____ but he will grow much bigger.

ball   call   fall   all   tall

hall   wall   small   stall   football

1.   dallounallerhallopuerll

2.   kallurallimurillostallim

3.   oallivalluiyallsmallion

4.   vallsterillutalluzallioter

5.   stralloplullaolluiwalloup

6.   flallourallaufallouflillert

7.   hoomellaopellfootballaso

8.   valluritoullopicalluijerell

9.   jallusperulliballuiyallirit

10.   alloipuyallivalluewuvalle

ball   call   fall   all   tall

hall   wall   small   stall   football

Crossword

all

Across

2. The baby's _____ was soft.

4. Not big.

5. A room in a house.

Down

1. I made a phone _____ .

3. _____ the boys like football.

4. A market _____ .

all   hall   small

call   ball   stall

Missing Words

1. It was _____ so I could fly my kite.

2. I had a _____ drink before going to bed.

3. My brother was _____ because I did not play with him.

4. The car windscreen was _____ and needed wiping.

5. It was a cold morning and the road was _____ .

6. The new loaf of bread was very _____ .

7. I gave my _____ some pink soap for her birthday.

8. All my friends wished me a _____ birthday.

9. There was _____ to eat at the party.

10. My _____ drives a blue car.

Mummy   Daddy   windy   misty   frosty

crusty   plenty   milky   grumpy   happy

Wordsearch

1. dridyujukyorilkyumilkyailp

2. MommyuMimmyoMummy

3. nistyubosvyoplentyuhurbeo

4. jindyuhilpyimistyubilkyugy

5. dontyihistyacrustyopilkyert

6. windyuhuchyidunbyovindy

7. DoldyDunnyiDeddyoDaddy

8. gostyukostyuhullyofrostyimy

9. numpyufumptyigrumpyivemp

10. jappyraltyeuhappyikappumdle

Mummy	Daddy	windy	misty	frosty
crusty	plenty	milky	grumpy	happy

Crossword

y (ē)

Across

2. Another name for father.

3. Another name for mother.

4. The ground is _____ in winter.

5. A _____ drink.

Down

1. The trees blew on the _____ day.

3. It is a _____ day and I cannot see far.

frosty   windy   Mummy

milky   misty   Daddy

Missing Words

1. We cut a new loaf of _____ for tea.

2. The shopping trolley was _____ to push.

3. We had bananas _____ of apples to eat.

4. The teacher _____ us a story.

5. I _____ the glue on the back of the paper and stuck it in my book.

6. Are you _____ to go to school?

7. Tim fell over and bumped his _____ .

8. In the race, Emma was a long way _____.

9. Do not _____ in the mud.

10. You must hold the tray _____ so that you don't spill the drinks.

head   read   ready   heavy   ahead

spread bread   instead   steady   tread

Wordsearch

ea (ĕ)

1. ceaduijeadiporeadivead

2. seadoipikeaduibreadiog

3. veadoadelinsteadujeada

4. reavyuheavyiogeavyuvy

5. ceadoigeadereafuheadiy

6. streayusteacenovyspread

7. ceadyuokeadyaureadyarp

8. deagyuveadyeadyusteady

9. aheadauryeacetaheaneavy

10. steafomeagautreadeageath

head   read   ready   heavy   spread

bread   instead   ahead   steady   tread

Crossword

ea (ĕ)

Across

1. The rock was too _____ to pick up.

3. I _____ a book yesterday.

5. John _____ butter on his toast.

Down

1. The part of the body that has the brain.

2. I cut two slices of _____ .

4. "Is tea _____?" I asked Mum.

read   head   heavy

spread bread ready

1. There was a huge _____ waiting to see the Queen.

2. We had both white and _____ bread for tea.

3. _____ many days are there in a week?

4. The _____ had a big red nose and a funny hat.

5. The Queen's _____ is kept in a safe place.

6. We went _____ the steps to get to the beach.

7. There are lots of shops in the _____ where I live.

8. _____ it is summer the days are getting very long.

9. The grumpy man always has a _____ on his face.

10. The _____ was munching the grass in the field.

cow   crowd   brown   down   town

how   now   crown   frown   clown

1. gowdarohoweaskoew

2. joweruyowobrowniow

3. yownusteowertownop

4. kowaronowirsfongowy

5. aowtocucrownarojows

6. ruwexowbikowucrowd

7. yowdertyuhocowihuxow

8. exowdiyuhomiwirudown

9. clownujowuedowiruyow

10. fowiropikowirufrownivew

cow   crowd   brown   down   town

how   now   crown   frown   clown

Name...
Date...

Crossword

ow (cow)

Across

3. An animal that gives us milk.

4. Not up.

6. A colour.

Down

1. A huge _____ was at the football match.

2. There are some new houses in our _____ .

3. The Queen wears this on her head.

5. Mum said we had to do our work _____, not later.

cow   now   town   crowd

down   crown   brown

Missing Words

1. The clock struck twelve and it was _____ .

2. It was dark outside but there was a _____ moon.

3. All of my work was _____ today.

4. If there is time we _____ go to the park.

5. The room was dark so I put on the _____ .

6. Sam has grown a lot so his shirt is _____ .

7. The old lady cannot read the paper as her _____ is not good.

8. Mum says that we can stay up later _____ .

9. The two boys had a _____ over who won the game.

10. The owl hooted in the _____ .

light   night   sight   might   tonight

right   bright   fight   tight   midnight

<u>Wordsearch</u>

1. vightucightasightpight

2. exightutonightougighty

3. spightujightaubrightiruy

4. skightionimightepoights

5. vightuyightebaightiright

6. migightofightuvopightey

7. foyightetightimubohightes

8. culightujightepightucighte

9. voghtmidghdightamidnight

10. wightolaghtounightereught

light   night   sight   might   tonight

right   bright   fight   tight   midnight

Name...

Date...

Across

2. The clock struck twelve at _____ .

3. A rainbow is a lovely ____ .

5. Not dark.

Down

1. Sam's jumper is _____ red.

2. We _____ go out after tea.

4. Not left.

right   sight   bright

light   might   midnight

1. Before going to bed we have a _____ .

2. Peter's watch had stopped so he had to _____ the time.

3. There was a _____ smell from the drains.

4. There are more boys in our _____ than girls.

5. The garden _____ needs sweeping.

6. At half _____ three we go home.

7. The _____ is long and needs cutting.

8. Jane came _____ in the race.

9. John's _____ is a fireman.

10. Mum said that the music was _____ loud.

bath   path   last   past   nasty

ask   grass   class   father   rather

1. palkuvathibathieleth

2. hastijastierrastoulast

3. catherovatherifatherg

4. fassousskirassergrass

5. kartyostenastyerstiyst

6. veskijeskobliaskosks

7. tatheroskihestharather

8. donassoclassijurasset

9. dastoiskijaspastivansk

10. tatholuthipathiothithu

bath   path   last   past   nasty

ask   grass   class   father   rather

Crossword

a (ar)

Across

2. Peter fell and came _____ in the race.

4. Another word for Daddy.

6. We had to _____ the way as we were lost.

Down

1. The garden _____ leads to a gate.

3. There was a _____ smell.

5. We would _____ go out than stay indoors.

ask   path   rather

last   nasty   father

Missing Words

o (ŭ)

1. _____ is at the start of the week.

2. Our _____ door is painted blue.

3. "Have you _____ your homework?" Mum asked.

4. The lady who lives next door has had
   a baby _____ .

5. We went to the shops to buy _____ food.

6. Sally's little _____ likes to splash in the bath.

7. In the holidays we went by train to _____ .

8. I asked if I could have _____ drink.

9. Sam's _____ bakes lovely cakes.

10. The _____ day I lost my pen but now
    I have found it.

mother   brother   son   other   another

Monday   front   London   some   done

1. vonutheromotherikoth

2. LononLodonirdLondon

3. contufrontilonmirothon

4. vitheryujothericathusch

5. vomekousomeiplomerin

6. eranoperanolitherianother

7. exineoponerivomedoneple

8. voniyokerousonitherobons

9. datherujitheroubrotheriney

10. MundayMenndayMonday

mother   brother   son   other   another

Monday   front   London   some   done

Crossword

o (ŭ)

Across

3. Another word for Mummy.

5. Not this way but the _____ way.

6. The capital of England.

Down

1. My _____ is older.

2. Jane sat in the _____ of the car.

4. My brother is my mother's ____ .

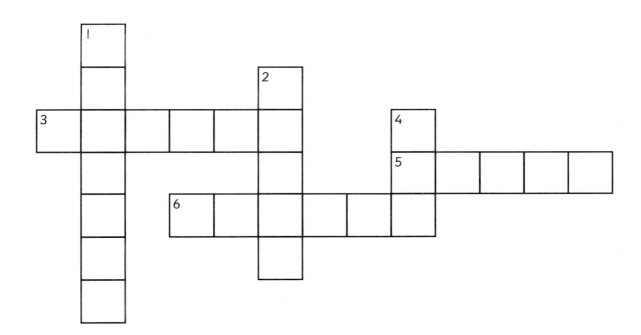

son   other   brother

mother   front   London

Missing Words

1. The little girl fell over and began to _____ .

2. I looked up and saw there were no clouds in the _____.

3. At school we _____ and do good work.

4. It is _____ so we can play on the field.

5. Dad likes to _____ eggs and bacon.

6. When it was dark the _____ fox crept into the garden.

7. "Have you seen _____ reading book?" asked John.

8. I asked the teacher _____ the sky is blue.

9. Mum told me to wait ____ the gate.

10. A big black _____ flew into the room.

cry	dry	sky	fly	my
by	try	why	fry	sly

Wordsearch

1. quiyopagryuskyileyol

2. vyujyouerthomyaropy

3. chyiolyunyioperiwhya

4. huryibryitryeryavoryer

5. fuyineryolewoyipofryt

6. snyoiklyiscyuflyujikly

7. dexuyodryiryecyisryush

8. vyuhisryujikyolyicryihir

9. nyuopokyunolyaubyicyt

10. chyuislyunerryubochyir

cry   dry   sky   fly   my

by   try   why   fry   sly

Across

2. I like to _____ eggs.

3. We went ___ bus
   to town.

5. The moon was up
   in the_____ .

Down

1. It is ____ pencil not yours.

2. The baby bird had to
   learn to _____ .

4. Not wet. ____ .

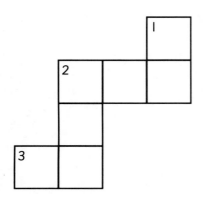

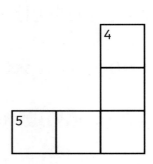

my   by   dry

fly   fry   sky

1. Emma has on a _____ skirt today.

2. The _____ was wide open as it was so hot.

3. The wind began to _____ the flag.

4. It was cold and _____ started to fall outside.

5. I had a seat in the front _____ to watch the play.

6. The seeds in the ground began to _____ .

7. I went to my friend's house so he could _____ me his new bike.

8. Some men had dug up the road, so traffic was _____ .

9. John needs some new shoes as his feet are _____ .

10. Jane jumped over the _____ wall.

snow	grow	low	slow	blow
row	show	window	yellow	growing

1.   quowurosfowotilowuy

2.   fudafowaneyellowirst

3.   gudowujowdowindow

4.   skowiyowisnowirtyow

5.   exowiryowablowablut

6.   fokinzowugrowikowurt

7.   mokoquowuslowopoew

8.   crolokowrowujowiftyer

9.   showuriyowaxowawole

10.   nopingugrowingolinkow

snow	grow	low	slow	blow
row	show	window	yellow	growing

Name...

Date...

ow (ō)

Across

2. Emma had to _____ out the candles on the cake.

4. White flakes that fall in winter.

5. A colour.

Down

1. The tree will _____ very tall.

3. Not high.

4. Not fast.

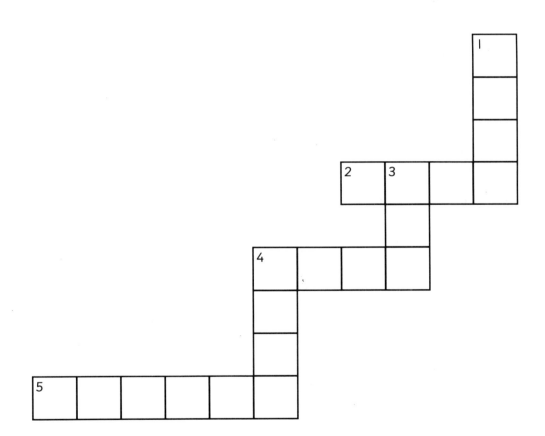

slow   blow   low

grow   snow   yellow